W9-BRD-154

Jackie Robinson

JUNIOR ▪ WORLD ▪ BIOGRAPHIES

A JUNIOR *BLACK AMERICANS OF ACHIEVEMENT* BOOK

Jackie Robinson

IRWIN B. BERGMAN

CHELSEA JUNIORS

a division of CHELSEA HOUSE PUBLISHERS

Frontispiece: In 1946, Robinson was a standout with the Montreal Royals, the Brooklyn Dodgers' top minor league team. Called up to the Dodgers the following year, he became the first black player in modern major league history.

Chelsea House Publishers

EDITORIAL DIRECTOR Richard Rennert
EXECUTIVE MANAGING EDITOR Karyn Gullen Browne
COPY CHIEF Robin James
PICTURE EDITOR Adrian G. Allen
ART DIRECTOR Robert Mitchell
MANUFACTURING DIRECTOR Gerald Levine
PRODUCTION COORDINATOR Marie Claire Cebrián-Ume

JUNIOR WORLD BIOGRAPHIES

SENIOR EDITOR Ann-Jeanette Campbell
SERIES DESIGN Marjorie Zaum

Staff for JACKIE ROBINSON
ASSOCIATE EDITOR David Shirley
EDITORIAL ASSISTANT Kelsey Goss
PICTURE RESEARCHER Sandy Jones
COVER ILLUSTRATION Daniel O'Leary

First Printing

1 3 5 7 9 8 6 4 2

Library of Congress Cataloging-in-Publication Data
Bergman, Irwin B.
    Jackie Robinson / Irwin B. Bergman.
    p. cm.—(Junior world biographies)
    Includes bibliographical references and index.
ISBN 0-7910-1771-0
    0-7910-2113-0 (pbk.)
    1. Robinson, Jackie, 1919–1972—Juvenile literature. 2. Baseball players—United States— Biography—Juvenile literature. [1. Robinson, Jackie, 1919–1972. 2. Baseball players.] I. Title. II. Series.
GV865.R6B47 1994   93-25170
796.357'092—dc20   CIP
[B]   AC

Contents

The first African American to play major league baseball, Jackie Robinson was among the greatest athletes ever to play the game.

1

The Great
Experiment

Play ball!" roared the home plate umpire as the
1947 baseball season began for the Brooklyn
Dodgers. Great excitement and interest filled the
stadium that day. It was the start of a new season
and the very first time in modern baseball history
that any American major league team had offered
a black ballplayer the chance to play. The player's

name was Jackie Robinson. And although many of the fans crowded into Ebbets Field that afternoon wanted him to succeed, there were plenty of others who hoped that he would fail.

Life in the 1940s was very difficult for African Americans in the United States. In certain sections of the country, particularly in the South, blacks could sit only in the back of public buses. There were separate drinking fountains for black people, and many restaurants and hotels refused to serve them. Many businesses would not hire a black man or woman, even when he or she met all the qualifications for the job. This kind of *racial discrimination* also existed in American professional sports. Not one baseball team wanted to sign a black player, even though many blacks had proved themselves to be talented athletes.

Before World War II, Jackie Robinson had attended the University of California at Los Angeles (UCLA). There he starred in many sports, including baseball. But Robinson had experienced racial discrimination in school and in the military, and he knew that things would not be easy in whatever kind of work he chose to do.

When the Kansas City Monarchs of the Negro leagues offered him $400 a month in 1945 to play baseball, Robinson quickly accepted. But he knew life in the Negro leagues would be very difficult. In many of the cities and towns where the teams played, African Americans were banned from the local restaurants and hotels. Black players often had to eat and sleep in the team bus. Robinson did not really want to play baseball in the Negro leagues, but he needed the money.

In 1945, Branch Rickey, president of the Brooklyn Dodgers, made a decision that changed baseball forever. Over the years Rickey had seen racial discrimination firsthand. In 1906, he coached the baseball team at Ohio Wesleyan University. When the team traveled to South Bend, Indiana, for a game, the hotel management found rooms for Rickey and all the players—except for the team's one black player, Charley Thomas. Rickey was outraged and persuaded the hotel manager to give Thomas a place to sleep for the night—on a fold-out cot in the corner of Rickey's own room.

"[Charley] sat on that cot and was silent for a long time," Rickey later remembered. "Then he began to cry, tears he couldn't hold back. His whole body shook with emotion. I sat and watched him, not knowing what to do until he began tearing at one hand with the other—just as if he were trying to scratch the skin off his hands with his fingernails. I was alarmed. I asked him what he was trying to do to himself."

"'It's my hands,' he sobbed. 'They're black. If only they were white. I'd be as good as anybody then, wouldn't I, Mr. Rickey.'"

"'Charley,' I said, 'the day will come when they won't have to be white.'"

Rickey never forgot that story and told it to many people throughout his life. After he became president of the Brooklyn Dodgers, he felt the time had come to sign a black ballplayer. But when he mentioned the idea to the owners of the other 15 major league teams, every single one of them disagreed with him.

In spite of the strong opposition to his plan, Rickey sent out several *scouts* to watch Negro league games. Rickey knew that many of his best scouts were from the South. Some of these men had deep racial *prejudice* against blacks. He was concerned that they might give him poor scouting reports on good black athletes if they knew that he wanted to sign a black player for the Dodgers.

Rickey also did not trust some of the other team owners. If they discovered what he was up to, he feared, then they might try to prevent the Dodgers from signing a black ballplayer. So Rickey made up a story. He told everyone that he was looking for players for an all-black team that he was forming, called the Brooklyn Bombers. The black athletes chosen by his scouts would play for the Bombers during the following season.

In the meantime, Robinson was becoming a standout with the Kansas City Monarchs. In 41 games, he hit .345, had 10 doubles, 4 triples, and

5 home runs. In fact, his performance at the plate and in the field was so spectacular that he was chosen as the starting shortstop for the West team in the Negro American League's East-West All-Star Game.

In spite of Robinson's excellent record, neither Rickey's scouts nor other black players considered him the best player in the Negro leagues. Rickey, however, knew that the player he chose would be watched very closely by millions of people. He wanted someone who would be respected off the field as well as on it. He also knew that a black player would have to take a lot of physical and verbal abuse on the field, even from some of his own teammates.

Before he made his decision, Rickey went to California to talk to people who had known Robinson when he was a student and an athlete in high school and college. The more Rickey learned about Robinson, the more he felt he was the right man for the job. In addition to Robinson's proven athletic ability, Rickey particularly liked what he heard about Robinson's personality and his educational background. He found out that Robinson was very intelligent and a good speaker. In 1945, Robinson was not married. Rickey was delighted to discover, however, that Jackie went out with only one young woman, Rachel Isum, whom he was planning to marry in the near future. Rickey also learned that Robinson played ball with a great desire to win and had experience playing with and against white ballplayers.

In August 1945, Rickey sent Dodger scout Clyde Sukeforth to watch Robinson play with the Kansas City Monarchs. If Sukeforth liked what he saw, he was instructed to invite Robinson to meet with Rickey.

On August 28, 1945, Robinson and Sukeforth entered Rickey's office in Brooklyn.

"I know you're a good ballplayer," Rickey snapped. "What I don't know is whether you have the guts [to be the first black to play major league baseball]. . . . We can't fight our way through this, Robinson. We've got no army. . . . We can win

*The complexion of
American sports changed
forever when Robinson
signed with Branch Rickey's
Brooklyn Dodgers on April
15, 1947. "Mr. Rickey,"
Robinson asked when he
first met the Dodgers
owner, "are you looking
for a Negro who is afraid to
fight back?" "Robinson,"
Rickey responded, "I'm
looking for a ballplayer
with guts enough not to
fight back."*

only if we can convince the world that I'm doing this because you're a great ballplayer and a fine gentleman."

Rickey paused thoughtfully before he continued. "Have you got the guts to play the game no matter what happens?" he asked.

"I think I can play the game, Mr. Rickey," Robinson replied. "Mr. Rickey," he continued after a moment, "are you looking for a Negro who is afraid to fight back?"

"Robinson," Rickey said pointedly, "I'm looking for a ballplayer with guts enough not to fight back." Rickey did not want Robinson to get into fights on the field. He knew that was exactly the type of excuse the other owners would use to keep blacks out of major league baseball.

On October 23, 1945, Robinson signed a contract to play for the Montreal Royals, the Brooklyn Dodgers' top minor league team. He won the 1946 International League batting title with a .349 average. When the 1947 season began, he was in the starting lineup for the Brooklyn Dodgers.

The meeting between Branch Rickey and Jackie Robinson had opened the way for blacks to play major league ball. In addition, it helped bring about changes in the laws of the United States for millions of other Americans who, like Robinson, were looking for equal opportunity in their work and in their everyday lives.

Robinson now prepared himself for one of the toughest challenges ever faced by an athlete. Many people were counting on him to do well. He had to try his very best and hope deeply that it would be enough to bring him success.

"I didn't know how I would do it," Robinson later wrote in his autobiography. "Yet, I knew I must. I had to do it for so many reasons. For black youth, for my mother . . . for myself. I had already begun to feel I had to do it for Branch Rickey."

In junior high school and high school, Robinson first
discovered his unique athletic abilities that would later
enable him to excel in collegiate and professional sports.
By the time Jackie joined the college track team at
UCLA, he was regarded as one of the finest young
athletes in the country.

2

A Rough
Beginning

Jack Roosevelt Robinson was born in a small farmhouse near Cairo, Georgia, on January 31, 1919. He was the youngest of five children—Edgar, who was ten years old at the time of Jackie's birth; Frank, who was nine; Mack, who was five; and Willa Mae, who was almost three.

Jackie's father, Jerry Robinson, was a share-cropper. He lived on someone else's farm and had to turn over at least half of the crops he grew to the owner of the farm. This required many long hours of hard work for very little profit, and after a while Jackie's father became tired of it. A few months after Jackie was born, Jerry Robinson told his wife that he was going to visit his brother in Texas. Jackie's father never came back home to his wife, Mallie, and the rest of the family. Years later, when Jackie found out the conditions under which his father had abandoned them, he was deeply hurt. "I could only think of him with bitterness," he confessed. "He had no right to desert my mother and five children."

"We never saw [our father] again," Jackie's sister, Willa Mae, told sportswriter Maury Allen, "but after Jack became famous he did show up one time. Jack didn't have anything to do with him and that was it."

Mallie Robinson now had to find some way to support her five young children. Shortly after Jackie's first birthday, his mother decided to move the family to Pasadena, California, where her brother worked as a gardener.

"As I grew older," Jackie later remembered, "I often thought about the courage it took for my mother to break away from the South. When she left the South, she also left most of her relatives and friends."

When the Robinson family arrived in Pasadena they moved into a run-down apartment that had three rooms and a kitchen. Jackie's mother and her five children slept in one room. Jackie, who was still an infant, and his mother slept in the only bed together. Jackie's aunt, uncle, and two cousins slept in the second bedroom, while another uncle and two more cousins slept in the third bedroom. Like many low-rent apartments of the day, there was no hot water and no kitchen sink. The dishes were washed in the tin tub that the family also used for baths.

Jackie's mother soon found a job ironing and washing laundry. However, she did not make enough money to support herself and her five children, and she was forced to apply for welfare money from the government.

"Sometimes there were only two meals a day," Jackie remembered, "and some days we wouldn't have eaten at all if it hadn't been for the leftovers my mother was able to bring home from her job. . . . My mother got up before daylight to go to her job, and although she came home tired, she managed to give us the extra attention we needed. . . . I remember, even as a small boy, having a lot of pride in my mother. I thought she must have some kind of magic to be able to do all the things she did, to work so hard and never complain and to make us all feel happy. . . . Her great dream for us was that we go to school."

Because Mallie Robinson had to go to work every day, Jackie went to school with his sister Willa Mae even when he was only four or five years old. Jackie was too young to be a student, but his mother asked the teacher to let him play in the school-yard sandbox while classes were in session. On days when it rained, the teacher took Jackie into the kindergarten rooms.

There were other nice people in the neighborhood who helped the Robinson family. The baker down the block gave the Robinson children bread that was left over at the end of the day. And the milkman would often come around at the end of his regular route to drop off a few containers of milk without charge.

In many ways, life for the Robinson family in California was better than life had been in the South. Black students and white students attended the same classes in school. There were no separate drinking fountains or public bathrooms for whites and blacks. There were no laws that blacks had to ride in special sections on trains or in the back of public buses.

When Jackie was old enough, he attended classes in the local elementary school. Many years later, he still fondly remembered his first teacher. "In kindergarten," he recalled, "I had a teacher, Miss Haney, who judged me as an individual and not by the color of my skin. She inspired me to believe that my chances for equal treatment from others were as good as anyone else's, provided that I applied myself to the tasks at hand."

But life in Pasadena was far from perfect. Along with other black people, Jackie and his family were forced to sit in a separate section of the local movie theater. Black children could only swim in the local pool on Tuesdays. The Young Men's Christian Association (YMCA) would only allow black people to attend its social and athletic activities one night a week. And many local restaurants refused to serve black customers.

Once when Jackie was sweeping the sidewalk near his house, a little white girl from the neighborhood started calling him names and making fun of him because he was black. Hurt and embarrassed, Jackie yelled back at her. He used all the bad words and insults he had learned from the other children in the neighborhood. When the girl's father heard Jackie, he stormed angrily out of his house. Soon the father and Jackie began to throw stones at each other. The girl's mother finally came out of the house and stopped the fight.

Like many of the other neighborhood children, Jackie had a lot of free time. Unlike many of his friends, however, Jackie put much of his time to good use. Along with his early morning paper route, he cut grass and ran errands for other families in the neighborhood whenever possible.

But even with all his hard work, Jackie still found plenty of time to get into trouble. "The rest of the time," he later confessed, "I stole all sorts of small things from stores, particularly food, and I was a member in good standing of the Pepper Street Gang. . . . We never got into vicious or violent crime, but hardly a week went by when we didn't have to report to Captain Morgan, the policeman who was head of the youth division. . . . All the time we were aware of a growing resentment at being deprived of some of the advantages the white kids had."

Fortunately, there were some special people in the neighborhood who cared about Jackie and helped him to resist the temptations of a gangster's life, which would ruin the futures of many of his childhood friends. One of the people who influenced Jackie during this period was Carl Anderson, an automobile mechanic who worked near where Jackie and his gang hung out. Mr. Anderson talked privately to Jackie about the gang, pointing out that if Jackie continued with the gang it would hurt his mother as well as himself. Talking with Mr. Anderson helped Jackie to realize that he was simply following the crowd because he was afraid of being called a chicken or a coward. From Mr. Anderson, Jackie learned that it took more

Baseball was not the only sport in which the young Robinson stood out. "The more I played, the better I became," remembered Robinson of his earliest experiences in competitive sports, "in softball, handball, football, basketball. . . . I played hard and always to win."

courage to stand on one's own and do the right thing than simply to follow the crowd.

When Jackie was eight years old, he discovered that sports were the one way that he could compete with whites on equal terms. Unusually big and strong for his age, Jackie first gained attention by playing soccer against sixth graders when he was still in the fourth grade. Soon he was competing in other sports against opponents of every size, shape, and color. Jackie was such a good athlete in elementary school that some of his classmates would share their lunches with him if he would play on their team.

Jackie slowly began to realize that his great athletic ability might be his key to a better life. "The more I played, the better I became," Jackie said, "in softball, handball, football, basketball. . . . I played hard and always to win."

Before joining the Dodgers, Robinson joined
the club's farm team, the Montreal Royals, where he
quickly became a favorite with the Canadian fans.

3

"A Glorious Challenge"

After Jackie Robinson graduated from Grover Cleveland Elementary School, he went on to George Washington Junior High and then to John Muir Technical High School.

At Muir High School, Robinson played on four varsity teams: football, basketball, baseball, and track. "I was also very much aware of the importance of being a team man," he later recalled, "not jeopardizing my team's chances simply to get the spotlight."

Robinson's coaches loved his competitive spirit. Some opposing players, however, felt that the best way to deal with Jackie was to make insulting remarks about his race and his family's poverty. They hoped that their words would upset him and cause him to lose his concentration during a game. But their insults often had the opposite effect. Jackie became even more determined and performed even better than usual. This ability came in handy years later when he played major league baseball. In his early years in the National League, Jackie was the target of many racial insults from other ballplayers who were jealous of his superior skills on the field.

Wherever he played and whatever the sport, Robinson was always a superior athlete. In one particular football game against Compton Junior College, Jackie was running down the field with the ball, with four Compton players barreling down on him. "He rolled one way, faked another," remembered Tom Mallory, Jackie's football coach at Pasadena Junior College, "and the four Compton guys crashed out of bounds onto our bench as Jackie ran in untouched for a score."

According to Mallory, Robinson's attitude and commitment to the team were as exceptional as his great offensive skills. "Despite all that individual talent," he continued, "he was quite a team player. He would block for the other guys, and he was a terrific tackler on defense."

The more Robinson competed, the more he excelled. During one school track meet in May 1938, Robinson long jumped 25 feet and 6 $\frac{1}{2}$ inches, a new world record for the long jump by a junior college athlete. That year, he also was named the most valuable junior college baseball player in Southern California.

One of the main reasons Robinson decided to attend UCLA after graduating from Pasadena Junior College was to stay near his family in Pasadena. Jackie was very close to his older brother Frank, and he hoped that by staying in Los Angeles he could "continue to benefit from Frank's encouragement." But Frank never saw his younger brother's great success at UCLA. In the spring of 1939, he was killed in a motorcycle accident.

Despite his great sorrow, Robinson enrolled at UCLA and became the first athlete in the school's history to compete on the school's four major varsity teams: basketball, baseball, football, and track.

In every sport in which he competed, Jackie's achievements on the college level were even more impressive than in high school. Claude Thornhill, the football coach at Stanford University during Jackie's college years, told newspaper reporters that Robinson was "the greatest backfield runner I have seen in all my connection with football and that's some twenty-five years." And Nibs Price, the University of California basketball coach, called Robinson, "the best basketball player in the United States."

At the time, Robinson felt that nothing in his life could be more important than his sports career. Then one day in 1940, when Jackie was a

21-year-old college senior, his best friend at UCLA introduced him to Rachel Isum, a freshman nursing student. Six years later, she and Jackie would marry. "I was immediately attracted to Rachel's looks and charms," Robinson later recalled, "but as in many love stories, I didn't have the slightest idea I was meeting a young lady who would become the most important person in my life."

In the spring of 1941, Robinson decided to drop out of UCLA only months before his scheduled June graduation. Although it was his mother's dream that he finish college, Robinson had come to believe that "no amount of education would help a black man get a job."

"I felt like I was living in an academic dream world," he later explained. "It seemed very necessary for me to relieve some of my mother's financial burdens even though I knew it had always been her dream to have me finish college." Rachel also wanted him to finish school. But Jackie was certain that he was doing the right thing, and he stuck to his decision.

Robinson soon found a job that he enjoyed, working as an assistant athletic director at a government-run camp for *disadvantaged* youth. There, he worked with many children who, like himself, came from poor or single-parent homes.

On December 7, 1941, Japan attacked the U.S. naval base at Pearl Harbor, Hawaii. Immediately, the United States entered into war against Japan and its ally, Germany. Millions of men and women were needed quickly to serve in the armed forces. Robinson was drafted by the army in May 1942. Because of his four years of college and his rare athletic ability, Robinson was accepted into Officer's Candidate School, an unusual position

Sports were the most important thing in Robinson's life— until he met a freshman nursing student at UCLA named Rachel Isum.

for an African American at the time. He became a second lieutenant in January 1943.

At that time, the U.S. Armed Forces *segregated* blacks into separate units from whites, a practice that disturbed Robinson very much. A proud and determined young man, Jackie refused to respect any rule or law that treated individuals differently simply because of the color of their skin. Many of Robinson's fellow soldiers were impressed by his courage in standing up to injustice. There were plenty of others, however, who were not accustomed to seeing blacks in positions of authority. To them, Robinson's behavior was arrogant and disrespectful.

During a brief tour of duty in Fort Hood, Texas, Robinson almost got himself thrown out of the army and into prison. One day while riding in a bus in Fort Hood, he refused to obey a bus driver who ordered him to "get to the back of the bus where colored people belong." Jackie was arrested and brought to trial. Eventually he was cleared of all charges of disobedience, but the incident soured his relationship with the army. In November 1944, Robinson received an honorable discharge for medical reasons: a broken ankle that he had suffered while playing college football.

Less than a year later, Robinson had his historic meeting with Branch Rickey. The result of the meeting was a contract to play baseball in 1946 for the Montreal Royals, the top minor league team of the Brooklyn Dodgers. Robinson was now just one step away from his goal—playing baseball in the major leagues.

Signing a contract with Montreal was a big step for Robinson, but it did not guarantee that he would play in the majors. Robinson knew that the Montreal Royals were a great minor league team. He would have to play at the top of his game under a lot of pressure to earn the chance to play for the Dodgers in the major leagues.

But baseball was not the only important thing in Jackie's life at the time. After a five-year engagement, he finally married Rachel Isum on

February 10, 1946, in a large church wedding. Two weeks later, the newlyweds left Los Angeles for Florida, where Robinson began spring training with the Royals.

During spring training, Branch Rickey was on hand for every game, giving advice and encouragement to Robinson. Signing Jackie was a huge risk, and Rickey wanted to be sure that his young star was ready. "Be more daring," Rickey shouted from the baseline. "Give it all you've got when you run. Gamble. Take a bigger lead."

In 1946, black fans were segregated in the stadiums of southern cities and could sit only in the bleachers and outfield seats. But they came to games in large numbers when Robinson played. Listening to the cheers and the thundering applause from the bleachers, Robinson felt a heavy burden of responsibility. He knew that all the black fans in the stadium were counting on him to succeed—to prove once and for all that black athletes could compete with white athletes on a professional level. But it was a responsibility for which Jackie was prepared. He looked at it as "a glorious challenge."

On the Royals' opening game of the 1946 season, Robinson showed that he was prepared to face the challenge. The Royals won the game easily, overpowering the home team, the Jersey City Little Giants, by a score of 14 to 1. Robinson was the undisputed star of the game. By the time the umpire called the final out, he had hit a home run, stroked three singles, scored four times, driven in six runs, and stolen two bases.

In spite of Robinson's quick success, however, he encountered many ugly racial incidents during the 1946 season. This was particularly true when the Royals were playing away from Montreal, where Jackie was a local favorite. Robinson was always very upset by racial hatred and the anger and insults he faced playing on the road. Years later, he declared that he had almost suffered a nervous breakdown during this period. He had insisted on playing every day, even—and especially—when the fans were most abusive. In Montreal, however, the fans respected Robinson, both on and off the field.

The Royals had a great season. They won the International League *pennant* by 19½ games and went on to capture the Little World Series of the minor leagues.

The Montreal Royals manager was Clay Hopper, a southerner from Mississippi, who was known to have deep racial prejudices. At the start of the season, the Montreal manager made no secret of the fact that he did not want a black man on the team. When the season ended, however, Hopper walked up to Robinson and shook his hand. "You're a great ballplayer and a fine gentleman," Hopper happily admitted. "It's been wonderful having you on the team."

Robinson's good fortune continued off the field as well. In November 1946, barely a month after the end of the season, Rachel gave birth to Jackie junior, the couple's first child.

It was only a matter of time before Robinson became one of the most popular players in the league. "When Robinson was on base," wrote Dodgers radio announcer Red Barber, "every eye in the ballpark was on him."

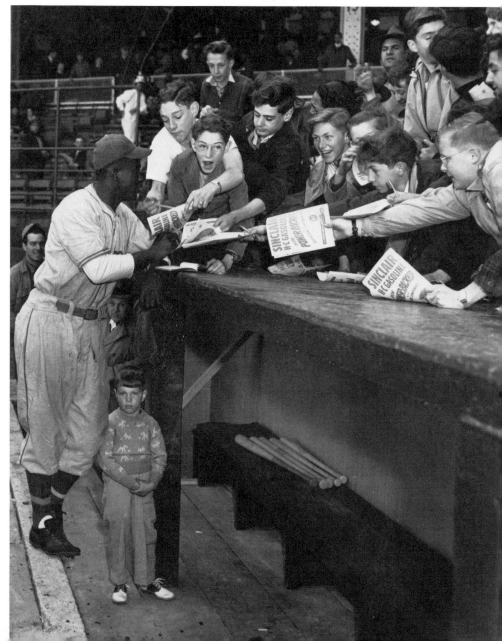

CHAPTER

4

The Heart of
the Dodgers

In January 1947, Robinson received a notice to report to the Dodgers and Royals camp in Cuba for spring training. He was instructed to spend his time at first base, a position he had not played in the past. Reportedly, the Dodgers were weak at that position.

Some of the Dodgers, however, signed a petition saying they would not play if Robinson was a member of the team. Branch Rickey called them into his office and threatened to throw them off the team if they did not tear up the petition, which they did.

Rickey felt that the key games for Robinson in spring training would be those in which the Royals played against the Dodgers. "I want you to be a whirling demon against the Dodgers," Rickey informed Robinson. "I want you to concentrate, to hit that ball, to get on base by any means necessary. I want you to run wild, to steal the pants off them, to be the most conspicuous player on the field—but conspicuous only because of the kind of baseball you're playing."

All of Rickey's advice and encouragement paid off. In seven exhibition games against the Dodgers that spring, Robinson batted a spectacular .625 and stole seven bases.

In spite of Robinson's incredible achievements on the field, however, some of the Dodgers still did not want him as a teammate. Rickey felt that Robinson had clearly earned a chance to play in the major leagues. He was determined to see that his bright young star got that chance, regardless of the racial *biases* of some of Robinson's future teammates.

On April 10, 1947, less than one week before the start of the regular season, the following statement was released to the newspapers: "Brooklyn announces the purchase of Jack Roosevelt Robinson from Montreal. Signed, Branch Rickey." Rickey offered Robinson a starting salary of $5,000.

Although Robinson had had a great opening game playing for the Montreal Royals the previous year, his first game as a Dodger—on opening day in Brooklyn, April 15, 1947—was not very impressive. In four at-bats against the Boston Braves, he went hitless, but the Dodgers won the game by a score of 5 to 3.

There were no racial incidents involving Robinson during the first few games of the season. This situation changed quickly on April 22, however, when the Philadelphia Phillies came to Ebbets Field in Brooklyn for a three-game series. Even before the first game began, Phillies manager Ben Chapman and some of the Phillies players began to shout racial insults at Robinson. Robinson did not reply. Before signing his contract, he had promised Rickey that he would not answer back to hecklers for at least two years. Robinson's teammates also remained silent.

Then in the last game of the series, Eddie Stanky, the Dodger second baseman, spoke up on Robinson's behalf. Stanky, who was a southerner, had seen and heard plenty of racial injustice over the years. Listening to the insults pouring from the mouths of the Phillies players, he decided that he had finally heard enough. "Listen, you yellow-bellied cowards," he barked at the players in the Phillies dugout, "why don't you yell at somebody who can answer back?"

"[Phillies manager] Chapman did more than anybody to unite the Dodgers," Branch Rickey commented years later. "When he poured out that string of . . . abuse, he solidified and unified thirty men. . . . Chapman made Jackie a real member of the Dodgers."

After the incident with the Phillies, things began to change in the Dodgers clubhouse. Along with many other teammates, Pee Wee Reese, the Dodger shortstop and team captain, began to show open support for Robinson, both on and off the field.

Now a welcome and confident member of the team, Robinson's playing really began to improve. During one stretch from the middle of June to the beginning of July, he had a 21-game consecutive hitting streak.

Perhaps the most colorful description of Jackie's play during this stage of his career came from Red Barber, who for years was the voice of the Brooklyn Dodgers on the radio. "Robinson on base—on any base, first, second, third—was the most exciting player I've seen," insisted Barber. "When Robinson was on base, every eye in the ballpark was on him."

The Dodgers did not have a great pitching staff in 1947, but they did have plenty of excellent ballplayers to thrill the fans and compete for the league championship. Among the standouts were second baseman Eddie Stanky, right fielder Carl Furillo, and first baseman Gil Hodges, as well as future hall of famers Duke Snider in center field and Pee Wee Reese at shortstop.

The Dodgers won the National League pennant by one game over the St. Louis Cardinals in 1947. Robinson certainly did his part to help them win. He played in 151 of the team's 154 games, batted .297, and scored 125 runs. In addition, he fielded well at his new first-base position and stole 29 bases. His daring baserunning upset opposing teams just about every time he got on base. At the end of the season, he received the first major league Rookie of the Year Award ever given by the Baseball Writer's Association.

The 1947 World Series pitted the Dodgers against a great New York Yankees team led by Joe DiMaggio, Yogi Berra, and Phil Rizzuto. Years later, Robinson looked back on that experience as one of the finest of his career. "My greatest thrill in baseball didn't come from any ball I hit, from any base I stole or from any play I made," he reflected. "It came when I heard the national anthem played just before the start of the 1947 World Series, my first World Series. . . . It was a history-making day. It would be the first time that a black man would be allowed to participate in a World Series."

The Dodgers played well in the 1947 Series but lost to the Yankees four games to three.

In 1947, Robinson was joined in the major leagues by four fellow African Americans: Larry Doby of the Cleveland Indians, Willard Brown and Hank Thompson of the St. Louis Browns, and Dodger teammate Dan Bankhead.

Robinson gained too much weight in the off-season and had another slow start in 1948. But he still managed to hit a respectable .296 by the end of the year. Unlike Jackie, however, the rest of the Dodgers did not recover their form by the end of the season. The team finished third, the lowest they would ever finish in Robinson's major league career. One "valuable development," as Robinson called it, was his shift to second base that year. Even though he would play other positions in the infield and outfield during his career, he usually did his best fielding at the second-base position.

Robinson knew he had finally been accepted in the league after being thrown out of a late-season game for heckling an umpire. "He didn't pick on me because I was black," Robinson later remembered proudly. "He was treating me exactly as any ballplayer who got on his nerves."

Another important development for Robinson and the Dodgers was the addition of the gifted Negro leagues catcher Roy Campanella during the 1948 season. A future hall of famer, "Campy" was a scrappy, hard-nosed competitor who would become a favorite with the Brooklyn fans. The combined performances of Robinson and Campanella over the next several years would be a key factor in the full acceptance of black ballplayers in the major leagues.

Robinson felt, however, that the most important event that happened to him in the 1948 season was being thrown out of a game for heckling the umpire. "He didn't pick on me because I was black," Robinson insisted. "He was treating me exactly as any ballplayer who got on his nerves. That made me feel great, even though I couldn't play anymore that day. One of the newspapers said it in the best headline I ever got: 'Jackie Just Another Guy.'"

Robinson's greatest year came in 1949, when he led the league in batting with a .342 average and won the National League's Most Valuable Player Award.

CHAPTER

5

Reaching
the Top

Many baseball experts consider 1949 to be
Robinson's greatest year. He made the All-Star
team, won the National League batting championship with a .342 average, led the league with 37
stolen bases, slugged 16 home runs, and drove in
124 runs. Playing in every single game, he collected
203 hits and excelled in the field at second base.
To no one's surprise, he was named the National
League's Most Valuable Player.

The Dodgers lost the 1949 World Series

to the Yankees in five games. Robinson batted only .188 but made a tremendous impression with his baserunning. "I had just never seen anything like him before," the great Yankee pitcher Vic Raschi said after the Series, "a human being who could go from a standing start to full speed in one step. He did something to me that almost never happened. He broke my concentration."

In 1950, Robinson once again hit over .300, but the Dodgers lost the pennant to the Phillies in an extra-inning game on the last day of the season.

Things were also going well for Robinson away from baseball. In 1950, his second child, Sharon, was born. And during the off-season, he starred in a Hollywood film about his life, *The Jackie Robinson Story*. With all Jackie's success, the family was finally able to move from a Brooklyn apartment to their own home in the St. Albans section of New York City.

Robinson had many great games during his career, but some say that his greatest was on the last day of the 1951 season. The Dodgers had to beat the Philadelphia Phillies again, this time in order to qualify for a playoff for the National League pennant against the New York Giants. In the bottom of the 12th inning, the Phillies had the bases loaded with two outs when Eddie Waitkus hit a blistering line drive that looked like the game-winning hit. But Robinson knew how important this game was to his team, and he was determined not to let the ball get past him. Without even having time to think, he dove to his left and somehow caught the ball. His right elbow jammed into his stomach, almost knocking him unconscious—but he still held on to the ball.

As Robinson hobbled off the field at the end of the inning, his teammates wondered whether he could still play. But Jackie soon put their fears to rest. In the top of the 14th inning—batting against Robin Roberts, an all-time great pitcher—he belted a home run over the left field fence. His blast won the game and put the Dodgers into a three-game pennant playoff against the Giants.

Only a few days later, Robinson showed

that he could lose like a champion as well as win like one. The Dodgers had just lost the final playoff game and National League pennant to the Giants in what one writer described as "one of the most bitter defeats in baseball history." Yet Robinson, upset as he was, walked to the office of Giants manager Leo Durocher after the game was over. "Congratulations, Leo, and good luck in the Series," Robinson said.

"That was one of the hardest things any man ever had to do, and I really appreciated that," Durocher later remarked. "Jackie Robinson had class. He was some man."

The Dodgers played superior ball and won the pennant in 1952 and 1953, but they lost the World Series to the Yankees both years.

Jackie's spectacular play continued to win the admiration of those around him. "There never was an easier guy for me to manage," commented Chuck Dressen, the Dodgers skipper from 1951 to 1953, "and there was nothing I asked that he didn't do. Hit and run. Bunt. Anything. He was the greatest player I ever managed."

Even Robinson's opponents began to praise his great ability and desire to win. Elbie Fletcher, a *veteran* player on the Pittsburgh Pirates, praised Robinson's "unbelievable reflexes. And [he was] alert, always alert." And Walker Cooper, a veteran catcher for several National League teams, said of Robinson, "He was just one terrific player. He was tough, he was fast, and he was smart. That's a pretty good combination for a ballplayer."

Robinson's teammates talked about him with great respect and admiration. "It was a thrill playing on the same team as Jackie Robinson," recalled Don Newcombe, the towering right-hander who was the also first black pitcher in the National League. "He was such a tremendous competitor. . . . I owe everything I have, everything I have in my life through baseball, to Jackie Robinson."

After breaking the major league's color barrier, Robinson was joined on the Dodgers during the 1948 season by two other Negro league standouts, pitcher Don Newcombe and catcher Roy Campanella. Newcombe would later recall, "I owe everything I have, everything I have in my life through baseball, to Jackie Robinson."

"Jackie would come up to me on the mound," remembered Don Drysdale, another future hall of famer who joined the Dodgers near the end of Robinson's career, "and say, 'Throw hard, don't let up, challenge the hitters.' He instilled a lot of competitive fire in my soul. . . . I admired him so much, worshipped him, I guess."

"When I first came up," recalled Carl Erskine, another outstanding Brooklyn pitcher, "I was pretty scared by the big leagues. I remember how friendly Jackie was. It's something you appreciate a whole lot."

In 1954, the Dodgers slipped to second place behind the Giants in the National League pennant race. At the end of the season, Robinson was still hitting a respectable .311, but he was slowing down. During the last four years of his career, he played in a variety of positions, including first base, third base, and left field. These are the positions where speed is often not as important as it is when playing at second base.

Going into the 1955 season, Robinson had

still not achieved one of his greatest ambitions. Despite his wonderful career and the extraordinary success of the Dodgers, Jackie and his teammates had never played on a world championship team. He was beginning to wonder if he might never get the chance.

During the 1955 season, Robinson began to show his age for the first time. He struggled at the plate for the entire year, batting only .256, the lowest average of his career. But baseball is a team sport, and the Dodgers squad played well enough in 1955 to win the pennant by $13\frac{1}{2}$ games. Manager Walt Alston and four of Robinson's teammates in 1955—Roy Campanella, Pee Wee Reese, Duke Snider, and young pitching sensation Sandy Koufax—had such great careers that they were eventually elected to the Baseball Hall of Fame.

The 1955 World Series once again pitted the Dodgers against the New York Yankees, their crosstown rivals from the Bronx. (Brooklyn and the Bronx are both boroughs, or sections, of New York City.) Postseason contests between the

Dodgers and the Yankees always created great excitement throughout the city and gave the winner bragging rights for New York. To the dismay of Brooklyn fans, however, the Yankees had won every head-to-head competition between the two teams in the past, including the 1947, 1949, 1952, and 1953 Series.

A team has to win four games to win the Series. The Dodgers lost the first two, even though an aging Robinson surprised everyone by stealing home in the first game. It looked as if it would be the same old story again, with the Yankees being crowned as World Champions. But the Dodgers came roaring back and finally defeated the Yankees in a seven-game series to win their first world championship. "It was one of the greatest thrills of my life," Robinson later said.

In 1955, after a long and much publicized search for a new house, the Robinson family moved to the all-white suburb of Stamford, Connecticut. Robinson's feelings on integration were clear: "I don't think there is any particular magic in a white kid sitting next to a black kid in a classroom. . . . I also believe both black and white children can gain something by being able to relate to each other."

In 1956, the Dodgers had another pennant-winning season, and it took the Yankees seven games to beat them in the World Series. Robinson, however, had slowed down quite a bit. He batted .275 and stole only 12 bases, while missing a career-high 37 games. He certainly still had base-ball ability, but he realized he could no longer play at the same high level that he had in the past. Jackie knew that it was finally time for a change.

An opportunity came at the end of the season when William Black, president of the Chock Full O'Nuts restaurant chain, asked Robinson to join the company as vice-president of community affairs. Robinson now felt it was time to decide whether to continue playing the game he loved so much or to move on to other exciting adventures in his life.

Robinson retired from baseball after the 1956 season and increasingly became involved in public life. He entered into the management of a restaurant chain known for promoting racial equality, and took an active role in the civil rights movement and other social causes.

6

Life After
Baseball

In December 1956, Robinson decided to retire
from baseball. Of the 1956 season, he admitted,
"I was benched a lot. My average was down, and
it was obviously time for me to leave the game."
But Jackie was not the type of man who was happy
just to sit back, relax, and do nothing now that his
playing career was over. There were many other
things that he wanted to accomplish in his life.

On December 10, 1956, Robinson accepted
the offer of Chock Full O'Nuts president William

Black to become vice-president of community relations for the large, New York–based restaurant chain. Jackie considered the company's reputation for promoting racial equality in making his decision. He knew that Chock Full O'Nuts did not discriminate racially when hiring workers. In fact, more than half of its employees were black.

Before Robinson had the chance to contact the Dodgers about his retirement, he received some troubling news of his own. The Dodgers front office telephoned him on December 11 to inform him that he had been traded to the New York Giants, the Dodgers' main National League rival, in exchange for $30,000 and pitcher Dick Littlefield. Robinson was "surprised and stunned." But the Giants were serious about their efforts to acquire Jackie. They offered him $60,000, a very large salary for a baseball player in 1956, especially one nearing the end of his career. They felt that Robinson still had the ability to play and that many fans would want to see him play alongside Willie Mays, their outstanding young center fielder.

Robinson, however, had always been a man with a great deal of honor, pride, and loyalty. "It would be unfair to the Giants and their fans to take their money," he told reporters. "The Giants . . . need youth and rebuilding. The team doesn't need me." Robinson never played professional baseball again.

During this same time period, Jackie was approached by the National Association for the Advancement of Colored People (NAACP), an organization whose goal was to bring racial equality to people in the United States. The NAACP asked Robinson to represent them in meetings with community groups around the country. They felt that as a celebrity, Jackie could raise a great deal of money for the NAACP and spread their message far and wide. Many people, black and white, would attend meetings simply to see the great Dodger star in person.

Robinson could balance his jobs—with the

NAACP and Chock Full O'Nuts—partially because William Black valued his commitment to civil rights and gave him the time off he needed for it. Jackie considered his work with the NAACP one of his great achievements and personally rewarding. "I started out talking for five or ten minutes at these meetings," Robinson remembered proudly, "and, when I got going well, I was doing half-hour speeches. . . . I remember the warmth and enthusiasm of those rallies."

Soon Robinson also had his own radio show. And in 1959 and 1960, he wrote a newspaper column three times a week dealing with issues he felt were extremely important: politics, civil rights, and international affairs.

In 1960, Robinson decided to become more active in politics by backing one of the presidential candidates: Vice-President Richard M. Nixon, a Republican, or Senator John F. Kennedy of Massachusetts, a Democrat. Jackie felt that Kennedy was a man "who knew little or nothing about black problems. . . . [Kennedy] admitted a lack of understanding about black people." When they met, Kennedy said to Robinson, "Being from Boston I haven't known many Negroes in my life."

"Having been a congressman all these years," Jackie retorted, "it should have been your business to know Negroes."

Robinson finally decided to support Nixon. He was impressed with the Republican candidate's civil rights record and felt that Nixon said "all the right things." Years later, Robinson admitted he had made an error, as President Kennedy proved to work for civil rights while in office.

Early in 1962, Robinson achieved the highest honor a professional baseball player can receive. He was elected to the Baseball Hall of Fame in Cooperstown, New York—a tribute reserved for only the greatest players and managers. Jackie's Hall of Fame plaque reads as follows: "Jack Roosevelt Robinson, Brooklyn, N.L. (National League) 1947 to 1956. Leading N.L. batter in 1949. Holds fielding mark for second baseman playing in 150 or more games with .992. Led N.L.

in stolen bases in 1947 and 1949. Lifetime batting average .311. Joint record holder for most double plays by second baseman, 137 in 1951. Led second basemen in double plays 1949-50-51-52."

Robinson's contribution went beyond statistics. As the first African-American major league baseball player, he opened the sport to all races, brought countless new fans to the game, and spoke out on issues of race.

At his induction ceremony in the summer of 1962, Robinson asked the three people in the audience who had meant the most to him—his mother, his wife, and Branch Rickey—to stand by his side as he received his award.

Later in 1962, Robinson became involved in a highly publicized dispute in Harlem, a large black neighborhood in New York City. Frank Schiffman, who was Jewish, wanted to open a restaurant in the area. Some felt that a new restaurant might hurt the business of a black restaurant nearby. Schiffman's most bitter opponents printed and distributed anti-Semitic, or anti-Jewish, signs.

This upset Robinson very much, and he spoke out. "How could we stand against anti-black prejudice, if we were willing to practice . . . a similar intolerance [against other groups]?"

Robinson became more and more politically active and eventually resigned from Chock Full O'Nuts in order to devote his time to politics. He campaigned for Governor Nelson Rockefeller of New York in the governor's unsuccessful

Robinson received his highest honor in 1962, when he was elected to the Baseball Hall of Fame in Cooperstown, New York. At his induction ceremony the following summer, Jackie had at his side the three people who had played the greatest roles in his life—his mother, his wife, and Branch Rickey.

attempt to win the Republican nomination for president of the United States.

After the 1964 presidential election, Robinson helped raise more than $1.5 million to start the Freedom National Bank in New York City. Many black business people had trouble securing loans from white-owned banks, which believed that black businesses were bad investment risks. The Freedom National Bank was formed to provide start-up loans to give black business people the opportunity to succeed.

For Robinson personally, the mid-1960s were full of sorrow. Within three years, two of the most important people in his life died—Branch Rickey in 1965 and his mother in 1968. In 1964, Jackie junior had enlisted in the army and in 1967, he was wounded in Vietnam. His homecoming in 1968 was not completely a joyous one.

For years, Jackie junior had been unhappy. Before entering the army, he had done poorly in school, stayed out all night, and had once run away from home. He and his father rarely spoke to each other and they were not on good terms.

In 1968, after returning home, he was arrested on charges of possession of drugs and carrying a concealed weapon. His choice was prison or a rehabilitation center. Robinson was shocked, and later reflected, "I had been so busy trying to help other kids that I neglected my own." He fully supported Jackie junior in his struggle to be free of his drug addiction.

Jackie junior was able to kick his drug habit, and after one year in rehabilitation he was released. Soon after, he started to work at the same rehabilitation center as a counselor. It seemed as if he was beginning to pull his life together.

Then, tragedy struck the Robinson family. On June 17, 1971, Jackie junior was killed when driving home from the center his car went out of control. Jackie senior almost collapsed when the police told him the news, but at the funeral, he saw so many ex-addicts whom his son had helped that he was comforted. He knew that Jackie junior's life had been important to many people.

Over the years, Robinson had developed serious health problems of his own. He suffered from *diabetes* and heart disease, both of which were gradually taking their toll on his health and his appearance.

One of his last public appearances took place in June 1972 at Dodgers Stadium in Los Angeles. It was the 25th anniversary of Robinson's first major league season, and the Dodgers were retiring the number of his uniform, number 42. Robinson's hair was white, he walked with a limp, and he was almost completely blind. But he was still there to show his respect to the fans and the Dodgers management and players—past and pre-sent—who were giving him this last great honor.

Just a few months later, on October 24, 1972, Jackie Robinson died of a heart attack at his home in Stamford, Connecticut.

"I have always fought for what I believed in," Robinson wrote in his autobiography. "I have had a great deal of support and I have tried to return that support with my best effort. However, there is one fact of my life which has determined much of what happens to me: I was a black man in a white world. I never had it made."

Jackie Robinson's ideas and values are kept alive today through the Jackie Robinson Foundation, a public, not-for-profit organization created by Rachel Robinson in 1973. It provides education and leadership development for minority youths with limited money.

"A life is not important except in the impact it has on others," Robinson often said. Jackie Robinson was much more than just a great baseball player. By succeeding in life against great odds, he set an inspiring example that has filled the lives of many people with hope and courage.

Further Reading

Adler, Davis A. *Jackie Robinson: He Was the First.* New York: Holiday House, 1989.

Frommer, Harvey. *Rickey and Robinson: The Men Who Broke Baseball's Color Barrier.* New York: Macmillan, 1982.

Robinson, Jackie, and Alfred Duckett. *I Never Had It Made.* New York: Fawcett Crest, 1974.

Robinson, Jackie, and Wendell Smith. *Jackie Robinson: My Own Story.* New York: Greenberg, 1948.

Scott, Richard. *Jackie Robinson.* New York: Chelsea House, 1987.

74

Glossary

bias   a strong feeling for or against without good reason

diabetes   a disease in which the level of sugar in the blood is too high; blindness may result

disadvantaged   lacking basic resources or conditions, such as standard housing, medical care, educational opportunities, and civil rights

pennant   a prize flag for winning the championship

prejudice   a strong feeling or opinion formed unfairly

racial discrimination   the unfair treatment of people based on the color of their skin or other physical characteristics

scout   one who recruits the best players to join a team

segregate   to separate some from others or from a group based on skin color

veteran   a person who has had long experience in a profession or an activity

Chronology

1919   Jackie Robinson is born on January 31 in a small farm home near Cairo, Georgia

1920   The Robinson family moves to Pasadena, California

1933   Robinson enrolls at John Muir Technical High School

1937   Enrolls at Pasadena Junior College

1939   Enrolls at the University of California at Los Angeles (UCLA); becomes the first athlete in the school's history to compete in four varsity sports

1942–44   Serves in the U.S. Army

1945	Plays Negro league baseball for the Kansas City Monarchs; meets Branch Rickey
1946	Plays with the Montreal Royals; his son, Jackie Robinson, Jr., is born
1947	Robinson plays his first game with the Brooklyn Dodgers on April 15; named Rookie of the Year
1949	Named Most Valuable Player of the National League
1955	The Brooklyn Dodgers win the World Series for the first time
1956	Robinson is traded to the New York Giants; he announces his retirement from baseball and accepts a position with the Chock Full O'Nuts restaurant chain
1962	Elected into the Baseball Hall of Fame
1964	Helps to establish the Freedom National Bank
1972	Dies of a heart attack on October 24, in his Stamford, Connecticut, home

Index

Irwin B. Bergman has received degrees from New York University, Columbia University, and Hofstra University. He is an associate professor on the faculty of the City University of New York. As a young boy, he saw many Dodgers games at Brooklyn's Ebbets Field. He considers Jackie Robinson one of the most exciting players he has ever seen. As a member of the Oral History Committee of the Society for American Baseball Research, he has interviewed many former major league baseball players. When not involved with teaching and with baseball, he enjoys hiking, music, and traveling.

Picture Credits